Underwater Animals

Text: Sharon Dalgleish

Consultant: Craig Sowden, Curator, Sydney Aquarium

This edition first published 2003 by

Mason Crest Publishers Inc.

370 Reed Road

Broomall, PA 19008

© Weldon Owen Inc.

Conceived and produced by

Weldon Owen Pty Limited

Library of Congress Cataloging-in-Publication Data

on file at the Library of Congress

ISBN: 1-59084-173-5

Printed in Singapore.

1 2 3 4 5 6 7 8 9 06 05 04 03

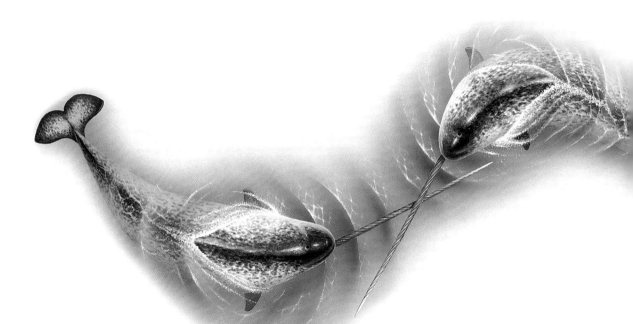

CONTENTS

LOOKING AT FISH

Fish come in many different shapes, sizes, and colors. Some are long and narrow. Others are short and round. The whale shark grows to eight times the length of a person. The dwarf goby is smaller than your fingernail. Some fish have bold patterns, and others are camouflaged. Some are even see-through!

1

2

AMAZING!

Scientists thought coelacanths had been extinct for 65 million years. Then, in 1938, one was found in a fishing net.

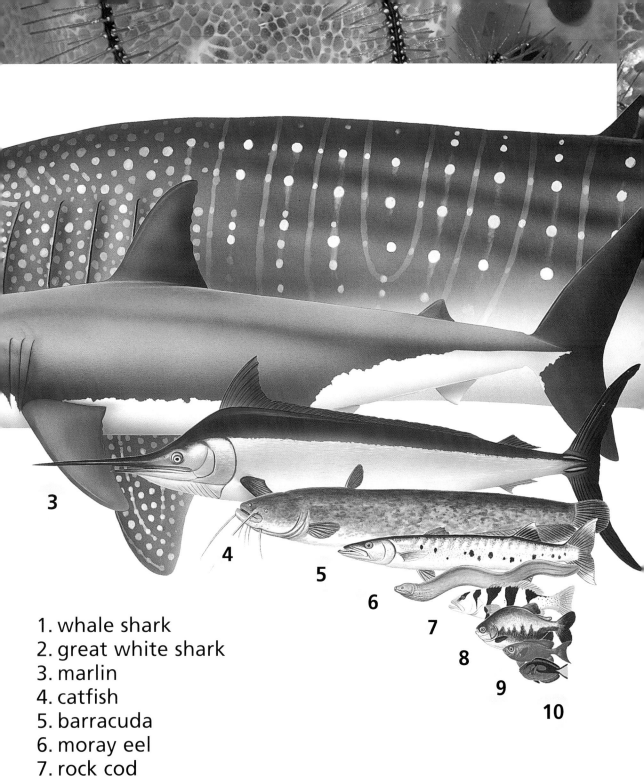

1. whale shark
2. great white shark
3. marlin
4. catfish
5. barracuda
6. moray eel
7. rock cod
8. paddle-tail characin
9. soldier fish
10. surgeonfish

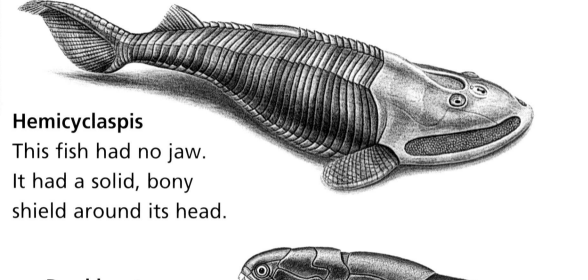

Hemicyclaspis
This fish had no jaw.
It had a solid, bony
shield around its head.

Dunkleosteus
This fish had a jaw,
but it had sharp plates
instead of teeth.

BEFORE DINOSAURS

The first fish lived 510 million years ago. Dinosaurs lived between 65 and 245 million years ago. Fish have been around much longer than dinosaurs! The very first fish didn't have jaws. Over millions of years, these early fish evolved into the fish of today.

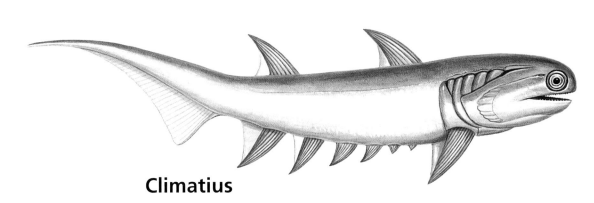

Climatius
This was one of the first
fish with a true jaw. It
looked a little like a shark.

DID YOU KNOW?

Toward the end of the age
of the dinosaurs, huge
marine dinosaurs lived in
the warm, shallow seas.

AMAZING FISH

Many fish have clever ways of confusing their enemies. The butterfly fish has what looks like a big eye near its tail. An enemy can't tell which is the front of the fish—or in which direction it will swim to escape. The colors on the black-headed blenny help it to hide in small, dark places. The moray eel has a long, thin body like a snake. It hides among the coral.

four-eyed butterfly fish

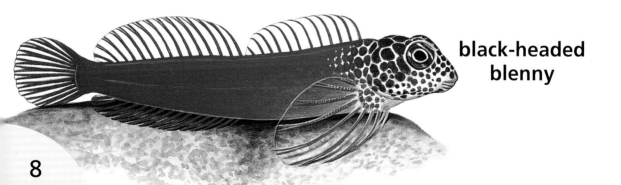

black-headed blenny

moray eel

CHANGING COLORS

Parrotfish start out as black
and yellow babies and grow
into brown females. Some then
change more than their colors.
They grow from brown females
into colorful males!

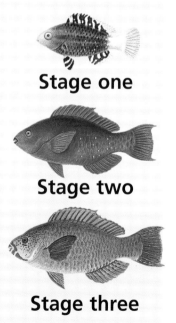

Stage one

Stage two

Stage three

Different fish have different tricks for catching their dinner. The gulper eel has a glowing light at the end of its tail. Any curious fish that comes to have a look is quickly swallowed in its giant jaws. The tuskfish has strong jaws to bite with and teeth like tusks. Often the hagfish doesn't need to catch its dinner. It finds a fish that is already dead, slithers inside, and eats it from the inside out.

DID YOU KNOW?

Most fish have small eyes. The southern roughy has large eyes because it feeds at night and needs to be able to see in the dark.

gulper eel

hagfish

tuskfish

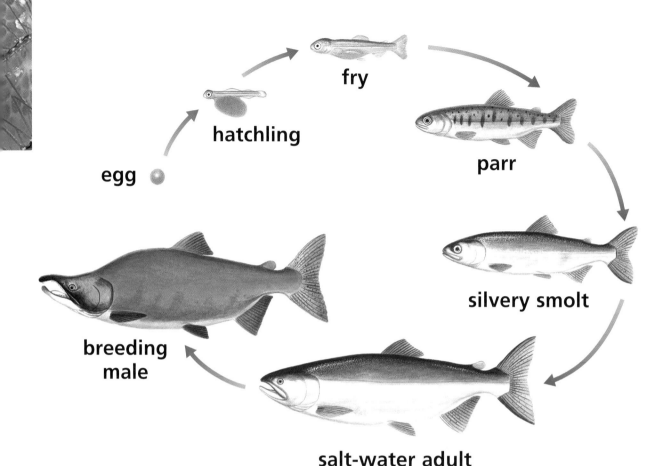

egg

hatchling

fry

parr

silvery smolt

salt-water adult

breeding male

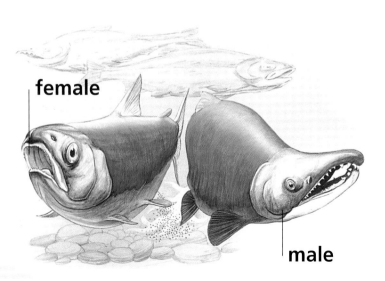

female

male

Life Cycle
When it is old enough to breed, a sockeye salmon turns bright red and green. The male even changes shape and grows sharp teeth.

Some fish make dramatic changes at different stages in their life. Sockeye salmon lay their eggs in streams. The hatchlings live in this fresh water until they turn a silvery color. Then they swim to the salty ocean. After about four years of living in salt water, the adult salmon change color again. They then swim upstream to where they were born, to breed and then to die.

STRANGE BUT TRUE

All purplequeen fish are born female. When a male dies, one female in the group changes into a male to take his place.

Unicorn Whales

The narwhal looks like a unicorn with its long tusk.

CURIOUS CREATURES

Some underwater animals look like they belong in legends. The narwhal is a whale that lives in the icy Arctic waters. When the male is about one year old, one of its teeth grows into a long, spiral tusk. Scientists think narwhals use the tusk to have sword fights! The sea horse is a fish, but it looks like a tiny pony, swimming with its head held high.

DID YOU KNOW?

Banded pipefish and sea horses are cousins. For both animals, it is the father—not the mother—that gives birth to the babies.

Horses in the Sea
A sea horse uses its long, curly tail to hang on to seaweed.

TURTLE TACTICS

The leatherback turtle is the biggest turtle in the sea. It doesn't have a hard shell like other turtles. It has tough, leathery skin on its back that makes it easier for it to swim and dive. Some leatherbacks die when they mistake plastic bags for jellyfish and try to eat them.

AMAZING!

The snapping turtle hides in mud at the bottom of streams, moving its red, wormlike tongue. Fish and frogs come to investigate and SNAP!—they're caught.

Sea Turtles

Sea turtles have strong front flippers to push themselves through the water.

FISHING FEATHERS

Many water birds can dive underwater after fish. Most have waterproof feathers that keep them warm and dry. The brown pelican uses its bill like a fishing net to scoop up fish swimming near the surface. Sometimes it also dives headfirst into the sea. Penguins are birds, but they can't fly. They have wings shaped like flippers so they can swim underwater.

HELLO, DADDY

Emperor penguin eggs are cared for by the male. He holds the egg on top of his feet until the chick hatches.

SEA OTTERS

Caterpillar Moves

Unlike other seals and sea lions, earless seals cannot use their back flippers to help them walk. On land they move like caterpillars!

FURRY SWIMMERS

Sea otters are furry mammals that spend most of their life in the water. They dive for sea urchins or crabs and bring them back to the surface to eat. They even sleep floating on the surface. Sometimes they come ashore in rough weather or to have their pups. Seals and sea lions come ashore to lie in the warm sun.

DID YOU KNOW?

Sea lions live together in noisy colonies. They bark, grunt, and bellow to each other.

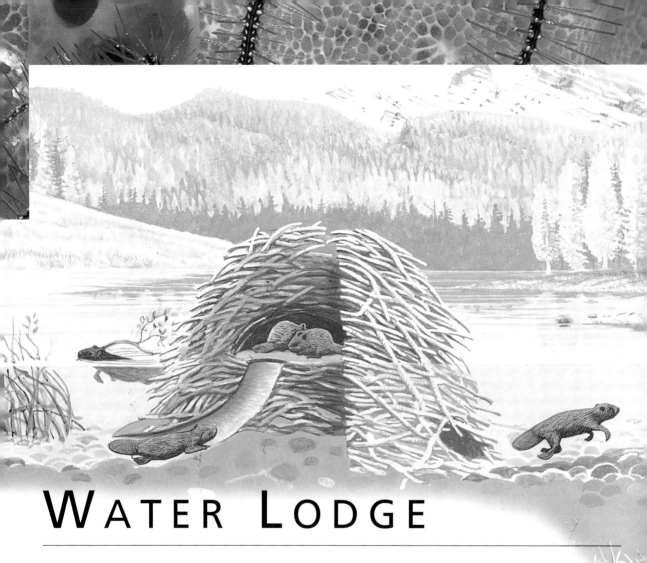

WATER LODGE

Beavers chew through trees with their gigantic front teeth and use the logs and branches to build a dam. This dam makes a deep lagoon, which the beavers use as their pantry. They pile branches under the water so they can eat them during the long winter. They also build a cosy home, with an underwater entrance to keep out land-living enemies.

AMAZING!

Beavers are great engineers. They know exactly how to arrange logs and branches to build a strong dam.

WHALE WATCHING

Whales are mammals, but they spend their whole life in the water. They have to swim to the surface to breathe, taking great breaths through their blowholes, which are like nostrils on top of their head. There are two types of whales: toothed and baleen. Porpoises and dolphins are toothed

Dall's porpoise

whales. Humpbacks are baleen whales. They don't have teeth, but feed on tiny sea animals that they strain out of the water.

common dolphin

humpback
whale

DID YOU KNOW?

Risso's dolphins are easy to recognize because they are covered in scars from playing and fighting with other dolphins.

SHARKS AND RAYS

Some sharks have streamlined bodies and are fast swimmers. Others have flat bodies and nestle in sand on the seafloor. Not all sharks have huge, jagged teeth. The whale shark is the biggest shark of all, but it eats by straining food out of water that it filters in its gills. Most sharks are not dangerous to people.

DID YOU KNOW?

People used to hunt the great white shark. In some countries, it is now a protected species.

Whale Shark
The whale shark is a gentle giant.

Blue Shark
The blue shark can bite a person.

Port Jackson Shark
The Port Jackson shark is harmless.

Bull Shark
The bull shark will eat almost anything, including people.

Rays have fins that look like wings joined to their head. They look nothing like sharks, yet they belong to the same class. Sharks and rays don't have any bones. Their skeletons are made of flexible cartilage. That's why they are so rubberlike. Your ears are made of cartilage, too!

Blue Skate
This ray has thorny spines on its tail.

Stingray
This ray has stinging spines on its tail.

DID YOU KNOW?

Chimaeras are relatives of sharks and rays. They are sometimes called ratfish because they have ratlike tails and teeth.

Blind Electric Ray
This ray can produce an electric shock.

GLOSSARY

baleen Long, strong strands that hang from the upper jaw of some whales. Whales that have baleen do not have teeth. Baleen is also known as whalebone.

camouflage Something in an animal's appearance that allows it to blend into its surroundings, so it can stay safe, or catch food.

cartilage Solid, elastic material inside an animal. Cartilage helps support the shape of some fish, like bones do in humans.

jaw One of the upper or lower bones that form the mouth and hold any teeth the animal might have.

mammal An animal that grows inside its mother's body before it is born. The young drink their mother's milk.

INDEX

PICTURE AND ILLUSTRATION CREDITS

BOOKS IN THIS SERIES